A First Cook[book]
for Children

Written by Evelyne Johnson
Illustrated by Christopher Santoro

DOVER PUBLICATIONS, INC.
Mineola, New York

Bibliographical Note

A First Cookbook for Children is a new work, first published by Dover Publications, Inc, in 1983.

DOVER *Pictorial Archive* SERIES

Library of Congress Cataloging-in-Publication Data

Johnson, Evelyn.
    A first cookbook for children.
    Summary: Fifty-five simple recipes.
    ISBN 0-486-24275-7 (pbk.)
    1. Cookery—Juvenile literature. [1. Cookery.] I. Santoro, Christopher. II. Title.

TX652.5. J62 1983
641.5 123   82-17759

Manufactured in the United States of America
Dover Publications, Inc., 31 East 2nd Street, Mineola, N.Y. 11501

Contents

Introduction

Cooking is not only a way to prepare food, it can be fun and creative also. Everything will be better, though, if you use good-quality ingredients, proper equipment, and follow a few basic kitchen rules.

Ingredients

Shortening. Butter and margarine can be used interchangeably in cooking. Where recipes call for salad oil, vegetable oil is meant unless otherwise specified.

Milk. Whole milk, skim milk or reconstituted dry milk can be used whenever milk is specified in a recipe.

Flour. Whenever flour is mentioned in this book, all-purpose unbleached flour should be used. None of the recipes requires that the flour be sifted.

Vegetables and Fruit. To be sure they have the greatest nutritional value and the best taste, fruits and vegetables should always be as fresh as possible. Remember to wash them before using.

Salt. Salt has been omitted from most of the recipes in this book because it is not a necessary ingredient. Should you wish, of course, you may add salt or other seasonings according to your own taste.

Equipment

All the delicious food in this book is easy to prepare using only the following basic kitchen tools and utensils.

Pots and Pans:
1-quart (4-cup) and 2-quart (8-cup) saucepans with tightly fitting covers
8″ and 10″ frying pans with oven-proof handles
9″ and 10″ round oven-to-table casseroles
Baking pans in assorted sizes and shapes. These can be used for baking main dishes as well as cakes. Some equivalent sizes are:
9″ round = 8″ square
10″ round = 9″ square
10″ round = 7″ × 11″ oblong
10″ square = 9″ × 13″ oblong

11″ × 15″ cookie sheet, preferably of a non-stick type, with a ½″ rim all the way around. This can be used to bake chicken, fish or pizza as well as cookies; but remember to use a plastic spatula with it to avoid scratching the nonstick surface
8″ loaf pan
12-compartment muffin tin with large-sized cups
1½-quart (6-cup) ring mold

Measuring and Mixing:
Set of standard measuring spoons
Standard measuring cups for both liquid and dry ingredients
Set of mixing bowls
Egg beater
Blender or food processor
Rubber spatula
Wooden or metal mixing spoons

Cutting and Chopping:
Assorted kitchen knives
Grater
Vegetable peeler
2″ biscuit cutter
Cutting board

Miscellaneous:
Vegetable brush
Rolling pin
Spatula or pancake turner—a plastic one for nonstick pans and a metal one for other pans
Pot holders
Minute timer that you can turn on as soon as something goes on the stove or in the oven. It is a good reminder if you get involved in something else, or are interrupted

Helpful Hints

For successful cooking and safety in the kitchen, always observe these simple rules.

Follow the Recipe. Always read through the entire recipe you wish to make and assemble all the ingredients you will need before you start to work. Most baked products such as breads, cakes and cookies depend for their success on a chemical balance, and recipes for these foods should be followed very carefully. When making other dishes, try the basic recipe first and then experiment with your own seasonings—remember to use a light hand because you can always add more later.

Measure Accurately. All measurements should be level and should be made with standard measuring cups and spoons.

Use Tools and Equipment Safely. Knives, peelers and graters are very helpful tools, but always remember to handle them with care because they can cut your fingers just as easily as they can cut the ingredients you are preparing. This caution is, if possible, even more important where blenders and food processors are concerned. These wonderful machines save a lot of preparation time and are great fun to use; but before you use a blender or a food processor, read the manual and be absolutely certain that you understand the proper (and safe) way to operate the machine.

Prevent Burns. Never let pan handles protrude toward you on the stove, always use pot holders, and be very careful when pouring hot liquids.

Prevent Falls. Always use a sturdy step stool when you have to reach for something on a high shelf. When standing on a stool, never lean over to the side to reach something that is just out of your grasp. Instead, get off the stool and move it right under the area you need to reach—it's worth a few extra seconds to avoid a bad fall.

Clean Up As You Cook. Wash your cooking implements before the food on them has become caked and dried. It is not only easier, it will keep your cooking area neat and pleasant to work in, and will avoid an overwhelming job later.

Sample Menus

Many complete dinners can be prepared using these recipes. Here are just a few possibilities—use your imagination to plan other menus.

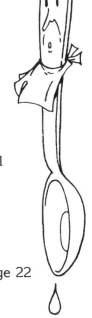

Meat Loaf Dinner:
Meat loaf, page 14
Scalloped potatoes, page 23
Mixed green salad, page 33
Strawberry shortcake, page 9

Chicken Dinner:
Oven-fried chicken, page 17
Carrot and raisin salad, page 34
Biscuits, pages 8–9
Chocolate cake, page 40

Ham Dinner:
Baked ham-steak dinner, page 21
Mixed green salad, page 33
Corn bread, page 10
Brownies, page 41

Fish Dinner:
Baked filets of fish, page 18
Baked macaroni and cheese, page 22
Waldorf salad, page 34
Carrot cake, page 39

Teen-Age Party:
Assorted crudités and dips (serve at least two dips), pages 26–31
Mini-pizzas (let the guests choose their own toppings), page 15
Variety of cookies, brownies, and cakes cut into finger-sized portions, pages 38–43
Homemade candies, pages 44–46

Muffins

These little cakes are made in special pans called **muffin tins.**

To make sure that the muffins don't stick to the pan, either rub a little salad oil over the inside of each compartment, or use paper or foil liners. Always preheat the oven to the temperature recommended in the recipe at least ten minutes before baking. Once the muffins are in the oven, don't peek for at least 15 minutes. If you don't have enough batter to fill all the cups, put water in the empty ones so that the pan doesn't burn.

Basic Muffins

Special Equipment:
Muffin tin with 12 large compartments

Ingredients:
2 cups flour
3 teaspoons baking powder
2 tablespoons sugar
1 egg
1½ cups milk
⅓ cup salad oil

Instructions:
Preheat the oven to 400°.

Put the flour, baking powder and sugar into a medium-size mixing bowl and stir lightly. Combine the egg, milk and salad oil in a separate bowl, add this to the flour mixture and stir only until all the flour is dampened— the batter does not have to be smooth.

Fill each greased muffin cup about ⅔ full. Then put the pan into the hot oven and bake about 25 to 30 minutes, or until the muffins are lightly browned.

Blueberry Muffins

Use the basic muffin recipe, but increase the amount of sugar to ⅓ cup and add 1 cup fresh or drained canned blueberries to the batter just before baking.

Cheese Muffins

Use the basic muffin recipe, but add 1 cup grated cheese to the flour mixture.

Biscuits

Basic Biscuits

Special Equipment:
Cookie sheet
Cutting board (optional)
Rolling pin (optional)
2″ biscuit cutter (optional)

Ingredients:
2 cups flour
3 teaspoons baking powder
⅓ cup salad oil
⅔ cup milk

Instructions:
Preheat the oven to 450°.

Combine the flour and baking powder in a large mixing bowl; set aside. Combine the oil and milk in a measuring cup (no need even to stir them) and add, all at once, to the flour mixture. Stir to make a soft dough.

For easy-to-make biscuits that will look somewhat like cookies, simply drop tablespoonfuls of the dough onto a cookie sheet.

To make more regularly shaped biscuits, transfer the dough from the mixing bowl to a very lightly floured cutting board and lightly press it together to form a ball. Then pat the ball of dough with your hand into a ½″-thick circle or roll it out to ½″ thickness with a rolling pin. Cut the dough with a lightly floured 2″ biscuit cutter (or use the greased and floured rim of a drinking glass), and then place the biscuits on an ungreased cookie sheet 1″ apart for crusty biscuits or close together for taller, softer biscuits.

Bake about 12 to 15 minutes, or until the biscuits are lightly browned.

Cheese Biscuits

Use the basic biscuit recipe, but add ½ cup grated cheese to the flour mixture.

Herb Biscuits

Use the basic biscuit recipe, but add 2 teaspoons chopped chives or 2 tablespoons chopped parsley to the flour mixture.

Orange Biscuits

Use the basic biscuit recipe, but add 2 teaspoons grated orange rind to the flour mixture, and substitute orange juice for the milk.

Buttermilk Biscuits

Use the basic biscuit recipe, but add ¼ teaspoon baking soda to the flour mixture, and substitute buttermilk for the milk.

Yogurt Biscuits

Use the basic biscuit recipe, but add ½ teaspoon baking soda to the flour mixture, substitute 1 cup plain yogurt for the milk, and also decrease the salad oil to ¼ cup.

Raisin Biscuits

Use the basic biscuit recipe, but add ¼ teaspoon cinnamon and ¼ teaspoon nutmeg, and ⅓ cup raisins to the flour mixture.

...and even Strawberry Shortcake

For a great dessert, cut baked basic biscuits across in half, top with washed and lightly sugared fresh strawberries or 1 8 oz. package frozen strawberries, defrosted. Serve with whipped cream.

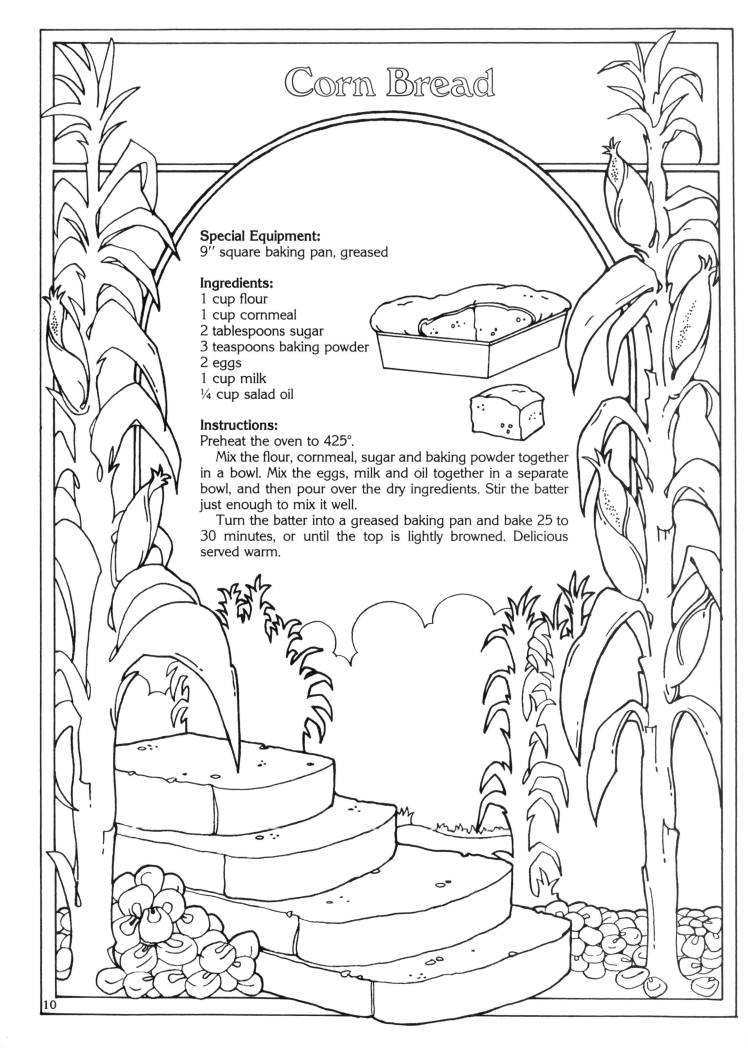

Corn Bread

Special Equipment:
9″ square baking pan, greased

Ingredients:
1 cup flour
1 cup cornmeal
2 tablespoons sugar
3 teaspoons baking powder
2 eggs
1 cup milk
¼ cup salad oil

Instructions:
Preheat the oven to 425°.

Mix the flour, cornmeal, sugar and baking powder together in a bowl. Mix the eggs, milk and oil together in a separate bowl, and then pour over the dry ingredients. Stir the batter just enough to mix it well.

Turn the batter into a greased baking pan and bake 25 to 30 minutes, or until the top is lightly browned. Delicious served warm.

Fluffy Baked Pancake

Special Equipment:
10″ oven-proof frying pan or casserole

Ingredients:
2 tablespoons shortening (butter or margarine)
4 eggs
½ cup flour
½ cup milk
2 tablespoons sugar mixed with ½ teaspoon cinnamon (optional)

Instructions:
Preheat the oven to 450°.

Put the shortening in a frying pan or casserole and place in the oven until the shortening melts.

Meanwhile, combine the eggs, flour and milk in a bowl and mix together until smooth. When the shortening has melted, carefully remove the hot pan from the oven and pour the batter into it.

Return the pan to the oven and bake about 15 minutes, until pancake is lightly browned. It will be a beautiful fluffy pancake.

Cut the pancake into wedges and serve immediately, right from the pan. Serve it plain, or sprinkled with sugar and cinnamon, or topped with fresh fruit or apple sauce.

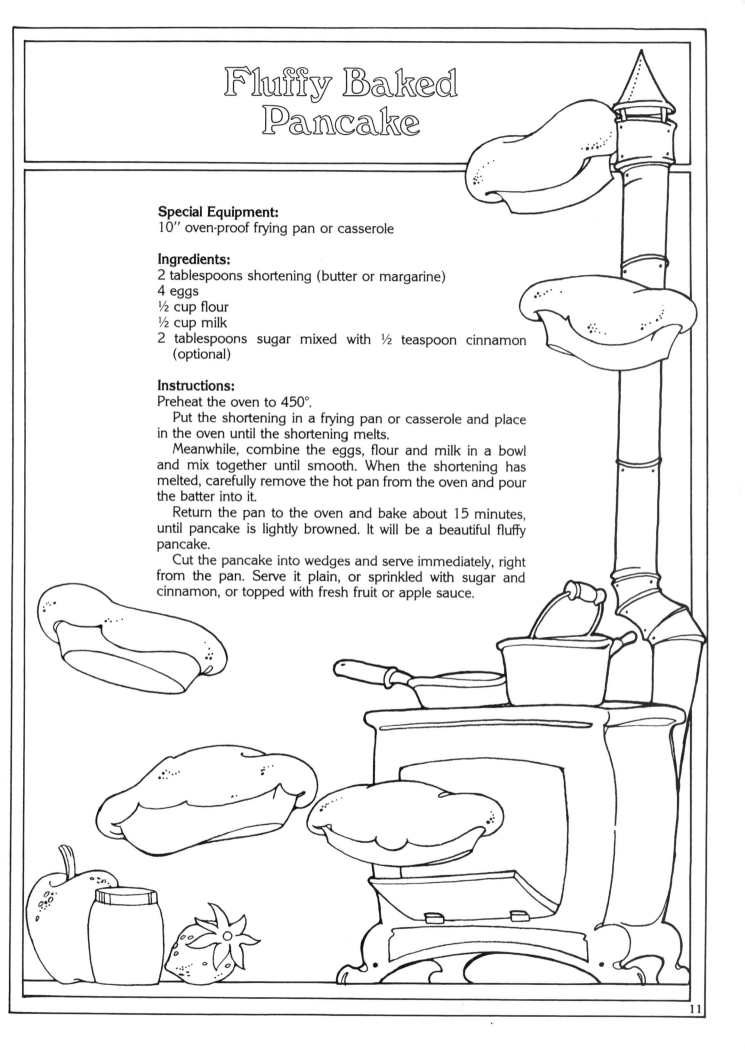

Basic Pan-Fried Hamburgers

Serves 4

Special Equipment:
Frying pan large enough to hold hamburger patties in a
    single layer

Ingredients:
1 pound ground beef
Salt for the pan

Instructions:
Divide and lightly shape the meat into 8 thin patties or 4
thicker ones.

Preheat the pan on the stove over high heat until it is
sizzling hot (at that point, a drop of water flicked into the pan
will jump). Then sprinkle the pan with salt, turn the heat down
to medium, and add the hamburger patties in one layer.

Cook the patties until they are brown on one side, then
turn them with a spatula and cook until brown on the other
side—about 3 or 4 minutes on each side. Exact cooking time
will depend on the thickness of the patties and how well-done
you want them prepared.

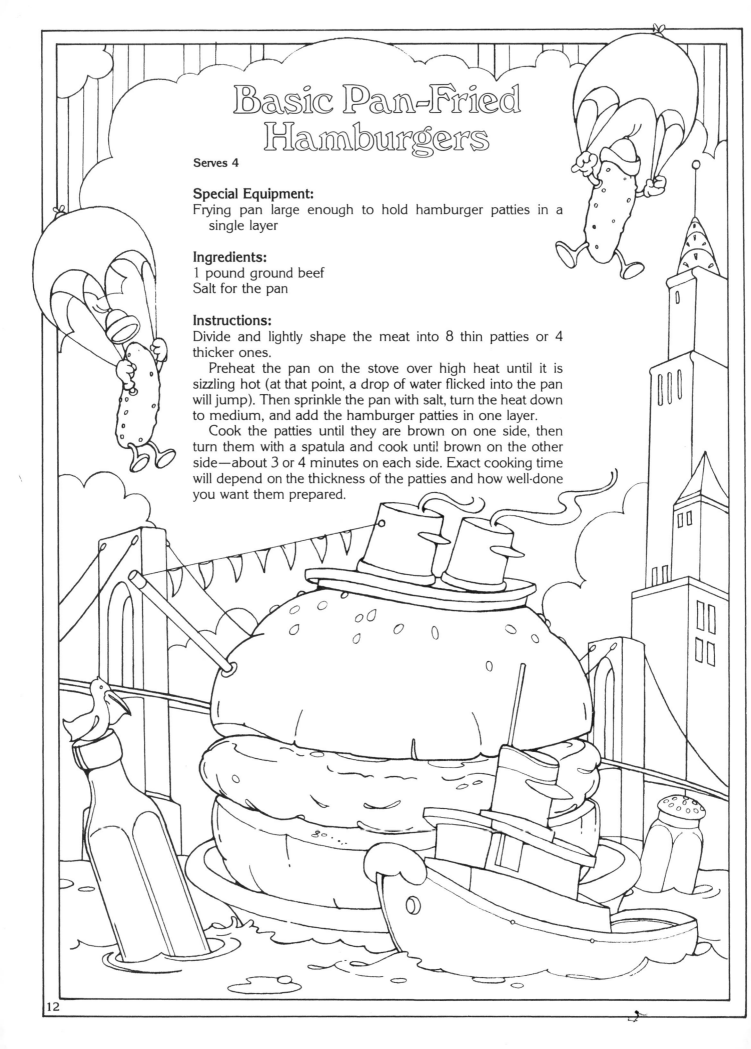

Cheeseburgers

Use the basic hamburger recipe but, after turning the meat to cook on the second side, top each patty with a slice of American, cheddar, Swiss or Muenster cheese. Continue cooking until the meat is done and the cheese melts.

Pizzaburgers

Use the basic hamburger recipe but, after turning the meat to cook on the second side, top each patty with a thin slice of tomato and then with a slice of mozzarella cheese, and sprinkle with dried oregano. Continue cooking until the meat is done and the cheese melts.

Meat Loaf

Serves 6

Special Equipment:
8″ loaf pan, ungreased or cookie sheet

Ingredients:
1½ pounds ground beef
1 cup uncooked oatmeal or bread crumbs
8-ounce can tomato sauce
½ cup chopped onion or 1 tablespoon minced dried onion
1 egg
1 teaspoon dried oregano

Instructions:
Preheat the oven to 350°.

Combine all the ingredients in a large mixing bowl and mix well with a fork.

Pack the meat mixture into an ungreased loaf pan or form into a loaf on a cookie sheet and bake 1 hour, or until the top is browned.

Remove the pan from the oven, pour off any fat that has accumulated, and let the meat loaf stand for 5 minutes in the pan before unmolding it onto a plate. Then allow the loaf to cool for 10 minutes before slicing it.

Mini-Pizzas

Special Equipment:
Cookie sheet

Ingredients:
4 English muffins
4 teaspoons salad oil or olive oil
8-ounce can tomato sauce or tomatoes, mashed
2 teaspoons dried oregano
1 teaspoon dried basil
8 slices mozzarella cheese
8 teaspoons grated Parmesan cheese

Instructions:
Preheat the oven to 400°.

Split the muffins in half with a fork, and spread each half with ½ teaspoon of the oil and 2 tablespoons of the tomato sauce or mashed tomatoes. Then sprinkle each muffin half with a little of the oregano and basil, and top it with a slice of mozzarella cheese and 1 teaspoon of the grated Parmesan cheese.

Arrange the pizzas on a cookie sheet and bake 8 to 10 minutes, or until the cheese melts.

Pizza Variations

Before baking, top each pizza with slices of pepperoni, cooked sausage, anchovies or raw sliced mushrooms.

Oven-Fried Chicken

Serves 4

Special Equipment:
Baking pan large enough to hold chicken in a single layer

Ingredients:
½ cup flour
2½- to 3-pound chicken, cut into serving pieces
4 tablespoons shortening (butter or margarine)

Instructions:
Preheat the oven to 400°.

Put the flour on a plate and then turn the chicken pieces in the flour until they are lightly coated.

Put the shortening in a baking pan and place the pan in the oven until the shortening melts. Then remove the pan from the oven, put the chicken pieces in it, and turn them until they are coated with the melted shortening.

Arrange the chicken pieces skin side down in the pan and bake about 30 minutes. Then lower the heat to 350° and turn the chicken pieces skin side up. Bake 15 minutes, then spoon some of the shortening in the pan over the chicken pieces and bake an additional 15 minutes—about 1 hour in all.

Baked Filets of Fish

Serves 4 to 6
Special Equipment:
Baking pan large enough to hold fish in a single layer

Ingredients:
4 filets of fish (about 1½ to 2 pounds), skinned
Juice of 1 large lemon
4 tablespoons shortening (butter or margarine)
Chopped fresh parsley

Instructions:
Preheat the oven to 350°.

Grease the baking pan and place the fish in it in a single layer. Sprinkle with lemon juice and top each filet with 1 tablespoon of the shortening.

Bake 5 minutes, then baste with pan juices. Cook a total of about 10 minutes, or until the fish flakes easily when tested with a fork—you don't have to turn the fish.

Carefully transfer the fish from the pan to a serving platter, using a spatula to prevent breaking. Spoon some of the pan juices over the filets, if you wish, and sprinkle with chopped fresh parsley.

Oven-Fried Fish

Serves 4 to 6

Special Equipment:
Greased baking pan large enough to hold fish in a single layer

Ingredients:
¼ cup milk
¾ cup bread crumbs or crushed corn flakes
4 filets of fish (about 1½ to 2 pounds), skinned
6 tablespoons butter or margarine, melted

Instructions:
Pour the milk into a shallow bowl and put the bread crumbs or crushed corn flakes on a plate. Dip each filet into the milk and then into the crumbs until both sides are coated. Arrange the filets in a greased baking pan and let them stand for 10 minutes to dry while you preheat the oven to 350°.

Bake for 5 minutes and then pour the melted butter or margarine over the filets. Baste with pan juices after another 5 minutes, and then cook an additional 5 minutes or until the filets are firm and golden brown.

Carefully transfer the fish to a serving platter using a spatula to prevent breaking.

Serve with tartar sauce (page 30).

19

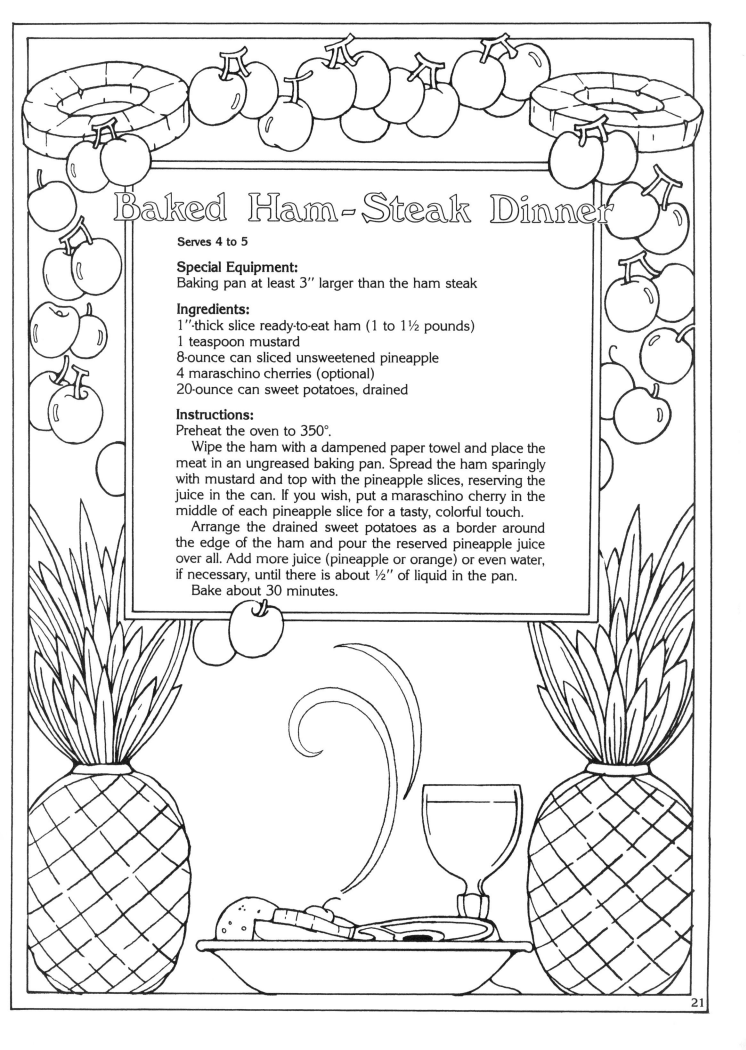

Baked Ham-Steak Dinner

Serves 4 to 5

Special Equipment:
Baking pan at least 3″ larger than the ham steak

Ingredients:
1″-thick slice ready-to-eat ham (1 to 1½ pounds)
1 teaspoon mustard
8-ounce can sliced unsweetened pineapple
4 maraschino cherries (optional)
20-ounce can sweet potatoes, drained

Instructions:
Preheat the oven to 350°.

Wipe the ham with a dampened paper towel and place the meat in an ungreased baking pan. Spread the ham sparingly with mustard and top with the pineapple slices, reserving the juice in the can. If you wish, put a maraschino cherry in the middle of each pineapple slice for a tasty, colorful touch.

Arrange the drained sweet potatoes as a border around the edge of the ham and pour the reserved pineapple juice over all. Add more juice (pineapple or orange) or even water, if necessary, until there is about ½″ of liquid in the pan.

Bake about 30 minutes.

Baked Macaroni and Cheese

Serves 4

Special Equipment:
9″ oven-proof casserole, greased

Ingredients:
4 ounces (1 cup) uncooked macaroni
1 cup shredded cheddar or American cheese
2 eggs
⅔ cup milk

Instructions:
Preheat the oven to 350°.

Cook the macaroni according to the directions on the box and drain.

Place ⅓ of the cooked macaroni as a layer in the bottom of a greased casserole, then sprinkle with ⅓ of the shredded cheese. Repeat the layers of macaroni and cheese until you use up the ingredients. Combine the eggs and milk in a bowl, mix well, and pour over the macaroni and cheese in the casserole.

Bake about 35 minutes, or until the top is browned.

Scalloped Potatoes

Serves 4

Special Equipment:
9″ oven-proof casserole, greased

Ingredients:
4 large potatoes, peeled and thinly sliced
1 cup shredded cheddar or American cheese
2 eggs
⅔ cup milk

Instructions:
Preheat the oven to 350°.

Place ⅓ of the sliced potatoes as a layer in the bottom of a greased casserole, then sprinkle with ⅓ of the shredded cheese. Continue alternating layers of potatoes and cheese until you use up the ingredients. Then combine the eggs and milk in a bowl, mix well, and pour over the potatoes and cheese in the casserole.

Bake about 1 hour, or until the potatoes feel tender when tested with a fork and the top is lightly browned.

Basic Rice

Serves 6

Special Equipment:
4-cup saucepan with tightly fitting cover

Ingredients:
1 cup raw rice
2 cups water

Instructions:
Combine the rice and water in a saucepan and bring to a boil. As soon as the water begins to boil, cover the pan and turn down the heat as low as possible. Cook over very low heat for about 20 minutes, or until all the water has been absorbed. Then turn off the heat and keep covered until ready to serve. Just before serving, fluff up the rice with a fork.

Rice Pilaf

Use the basic rice recipe but, when combining the rice and water in the saucepan, add ¼ cup slivered almonds, ¼ cup raisins and ½ teaspoon cinnamon.

Crudités

Pronounced "Croo-dit-tays"

This pretty French word means a variety of raw vegetables that are cut into small pieces. In France, crudités are often tossed with a little salad dressing (pages 36-37) and served as a salad course; but here raw vegetables are usually used plain as snacks, or with a variety of dips (pages 28-31). Be sure to buy the freshest vegetables you can get and use them as soon as possible.

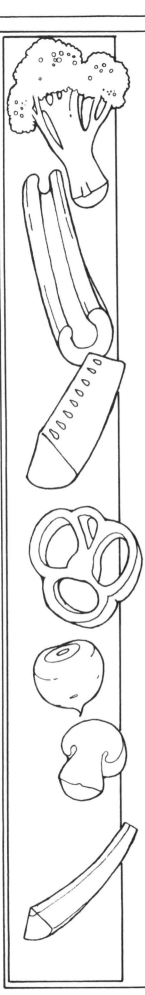

Preparation and Storage:

Broccoli. Cut off the large leaves and the tough portions of the stalks and discard them. Then cut the flowerets apart, leaving them attached to 2″ to 3″ of the thin stems. Rinse well and store in a bowl of water in the refrigerator.

Carrots. Cut off the green tops and discard them. Scrub the carrots well with a vegetable brush or peel them with a vegetable peeler. Then cut them into strips and store in a bowl of water in the refrigerator.

Cauliflower. Remove the outer leaves and the stem and discard. Trim away any blemished portions of the flowerets. Separate the flowerets, rinse them well, and then store in a bowl of water in the refrigerator.

Celery. Remove and discard the leaves, then separate the stalks and rinse them well. If the stalks are large, cut them lengthwise into 1″-wide strips and then cut the strips into 3″- to 4″-long pieces. To store, just stand the celery pieces in a glass of water in the refrigerator, or put them into a bowl with any of the other vegetables that are being stored in water.

Cherry Tomatoes. Wash and dry well with paper towels, and then store uncovered in the refrigerator until ready to use.

Cucumbers. Peel the cucumbers with a vegetable peeler, cut them in half lengthwise and then cut again into long strips. Slice the strips in half, if desired, and then wrap them in foil or plastic wrap and store in the refrigerator.

Green or Red Peppers. Trim off a thin slice from the stem end of the peppers and then cut out the seeds and the fibrous center portion. Wash well, inside and out, and cut into strips or rings. Store in plastic bag or container in the refrigerator.

Mushrooms. Wipe with a dampened paper towel and sprinkle them with lemon juice to prevent discoloring. Store in a plastic bag or in a dish covered with plastic wrap or foil, and refrigerate.

Radishes. Trim off the leaves and stems and cut away any blemishes. Wash the radishes well and then store them in a bowl of water in the refrigerator.

String Beans. Wash the beans well, cut off the stem ends and remove any blemishes. Then wrap the beans in foil or plastic wrap and store in the refrigerator.

Zucchini. Scrub well, but do not peel. Trim off and discard the stem and blossom ends, cut the zucchini in half length-wise, and then cut into long strips. Slice the strips in half, if desired, and then wrap them in foil or plastic wrap and store in the refrigerator.

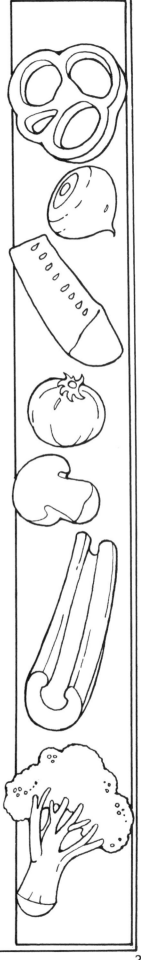

Dips and Dunks

All these dips can easily be mixed right in a bowl. Just combine the ingredients, stir well, then cover and refrigerate until serving time.

Pizza Dip

1 cup sour cream
2 tablespoons catsup
2 tablespoons minced dried onion
1 teaspoon dried basil
1 teaspoon dried oregano

Soy Dip

1 cup mayonnaise
5 teaspoons soy sauce
1 tablespoon minced dried onion
2 teaspoons vinegar
½ teaspoon ground ginger

Curry Dip

1 cup mayonnaise
2 tablespoons curry powder
1 tablespoon lemon juice
1 clove garlic, crushed, or garlic
    powder to taste

Horseradish Dip

1 cup sour cream
1 to 2 tablespoons prepared white
    horseradish, or to taste

Onion Dip

1 cup sour cream
½ package dried onion soup mix

Dips and Dunks

Clam Dip

1 cup sour cream or plain yogurt
6½-ounce can minced clams, drained
2 tablespoons minced dried onion
1 tablespoon lemon juice

Mustard Dip

1 cup mayonnaise
1 teaspoon mustard
½ teaspoon curry powder (optional)
Freshly ground pepper to taste

Herb Dip

1 cup cottage cheese
6 sprigs fresh parsley
2 small scallions, white part and all

Tartar Sauce

1 cup mayonnaise
1 tablespoon chopped sweet pickle or pickle relish
1 tablespoon lemon juice
1 clove garlic, crushed

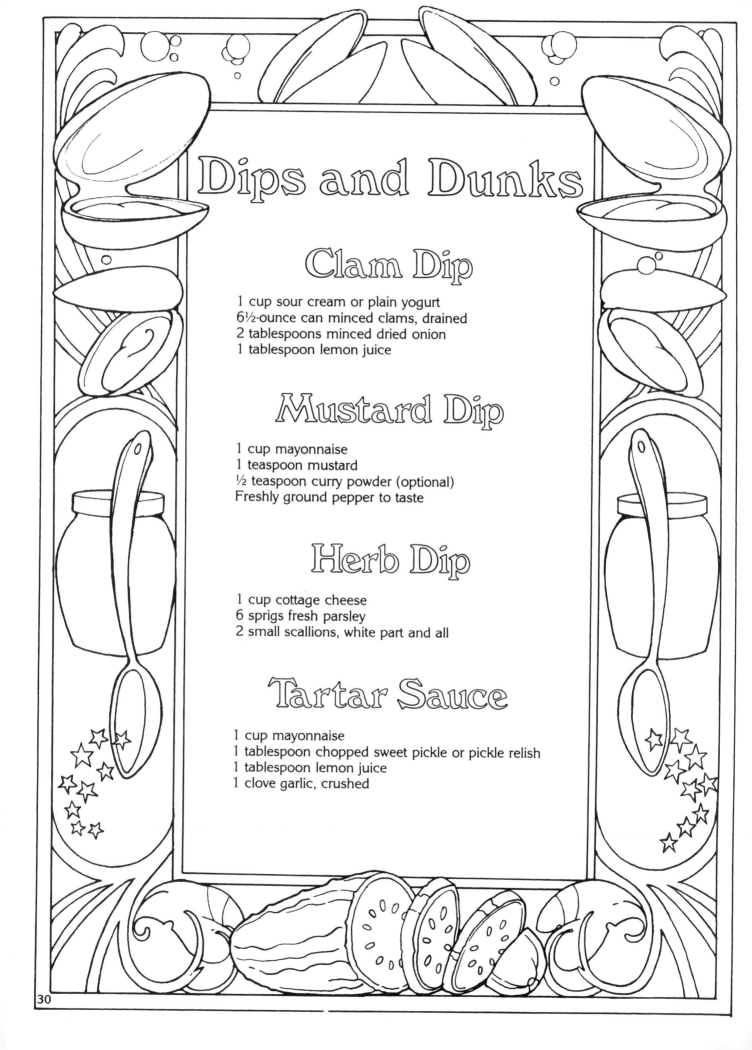

These dips are quick and easy to make if you have a blender or food processor—just be sure you know how to operate the machine properly. Combine the ingredients in the container of the blender or food processor, whirl until smooth and store in a bowl in the refrigerator until serving time.

Chutney Dip

1 cup cottage cheese
¼ cup chutney

Mexicali Dip

1 cup cottage cheese
3 tablespoons chili sauce
1 tablespoon lemon juice

Tuna Dip

6½-ounce can tuna, drained
2 tablespoons mayonnaise
2 tablespoons catsup
1 tablespoon lemon juice

Mixed Green Salad

Preparation and Storage:
Always use the freshest and best-quality vegetables you can get. To prepare lettuce and other salad greens (such as Bibb or romaine lettuce, chicory and spinach), separate the leaves and wash them carefully in cold water. Discard any blemished or discolored parts. Dry the greens thoroughly with paper towels and then put them in an airtight plastic bag or container. Store in the refrigerator so that the greens will be chilled and crisp when ready to eat.

Serving:
Use a large bowl to mix the salad. Tear the greens into bite-sized pieces right into the bowl. You can figure about 1½ cups of salad per person.

Choose a salad dressing (pages 36–37), and just before serving, mix the salad with just enough dressing to lightly coat all the greens.

Colorful Tossed Salad

Be as creative as possible. Combine several different kinds of greens in a large bowl, and then add as many of the following ingredients as you wish:

Thinly sliced onion
Chopped fresh parsley
Cubed or sliced tomatoes
Peeled and sliced or diced avocado
Shredded red cabbage
Grated cheese
Selected crudités (pages 26–27), cut into bite-sized pieces

Just before serving, toss with a salad dressing of your choice (pages 36–37), using just enough dressing to lightly coat the ingredients.

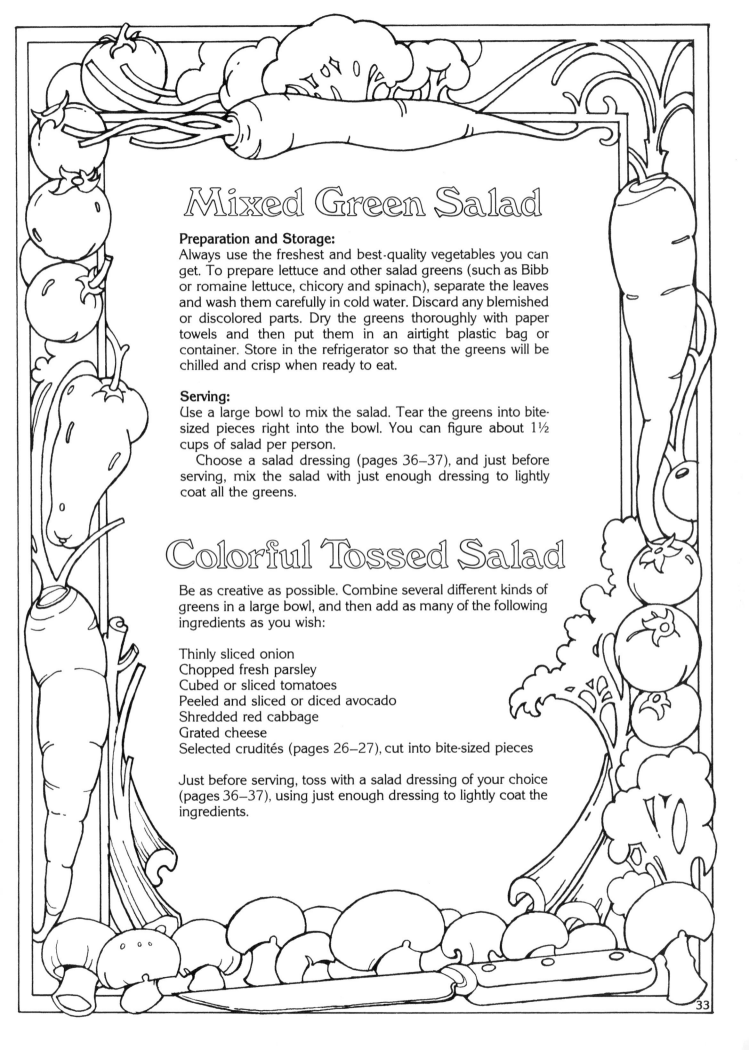

Chef's Salad

A meal in itself, this delicious dish is especially good for lunch or dinner on a warm summer day. To make it, use the tossed salad recipe, but add diced ham, diced turkey, cubed cheese and sliced hard-boiled eggs.

Carrot and Raisin Salad

Serves 4

Ingredients:
4 large carrots, grated
1 cup raisins
½ cup mayonnaise (approximately)

Instructions:
Combine the grated carrots and raisins in a bowl and stir in just enough mayonnaise to moisten. Cover the bowl and keep the salad refrigerated until serving time.

Waldorf Salad

Serves 4

Ingredients:
4 medium-sized apples, cored and diced
4 celery stalks, diced
½ cup chopped walnuts
½ cup raisins
½ cup mayonnaise (approximately)
2 teaspoons lemon juice

Instructions:
Combine all the ingredients in a bowl. Cover and refrigerate until serving time.

Tomato Aspic Salad

Serves 8

Special Equipment:
8-cup saucepan
6-cup ring mold, well greased
Flat serving platter at least 1″ larger than the ring mold

Ingredients:
2 envelopes (2 tablespoons) unflavored gelatin
2 cups cold water
15-ounce can tomato sauce
1 tablespoon lemon juice
2 cups cottage cheese
2 tablespoons chopped scallions or chives

Instructions:
Put the gelatin into a saucepan, moisten it with ½ cup of the water, and then add the remaining 1½ cups of water. Place the saucepan on the stove and stir over low heat just until the gelatin is dissolved. Do not let the mixture come to a boil.

Remove the pan from the heat and stir in the tomato sauce and lemon juice. Pour the liquid into a greased ring mold and chill in the refrigerator until firm.

To unmold the aspic, quickly dip the pan right up to the rim in a sink full of hot water. Then invert the mold onto a perfectly flat serving platter so that the aspic will not crack.

Just before serving, fill the center of the aspic with cottage cheese and sprinkle with chopped scallions or chives.
Serve with Russian dressing (page 37) on the side.

Salad Dressings

Mayonnaise

Makes about 1¼ cups

Special Equipment:
If you have a blender or a food processor, it's fun and easy to make your own mayonnaise. Just be sure that you know how to use the machine properly.

Ingredients:
1 egg
1 teaspoon mustard
1 tablespoon lemon juice or vinegar
1 cup salad oil (not olive oil)

Instructions:
Break the egg into the container of a blender or food processor. Add the mustard and the lemon juice or vinegar, and turn on the machine. With the machine running, pour the salad oil into the container very, very slowly. By the time you have poured in all the oil, the mayonnaise will be nice and thick. Turn off the machine and put the mayonnaise into a clean jar. Store tightly covered in the refrigerator.

Russian Dressing

To 1 cup mayonnaise (either homemade or bought), add about ½ cup chili sauce or catsup. Stir until the ingredients are well mixed, then store in the refrigerator in a tightly covered jar.

Watercress Dressing

Thoroughly wash about ¼ cup watercress in cold water, then dry with paper towels. Chop the watercress, stems and all, and add to 1 cup mayonnaise. Stir until the ingredients are well mixed and refrigerate in a tightly covered jar.

Thousand Island Dressing

To 1 cup mayonnaise, add 1 chopped hard-boiled egg, 3 tablespoons chili sauce or catsup and 2 tablespoons chopped pickles or olives. Mix well, and then refrigerate in a tightly covered jar.

French Dressing

Combine ⅔ cup salad oil or olive oil, ⅓ cup lemon juice or vinegar, 1 clove garlic and ½ teaspoon dry mustard in a 2-cup jar with a tightly fitting cover. Shake well and refrigerate until you are ready to use. Shake well again just before serving.

Fresh Apple Cake

Special Equipment:
9″ × 13″ oblong or 10″ square baking pan, greased

Ingredients:
1½ cups flour
1 teaspoon baking soda
¾ cup sugar
1 teaspoon cinnamon
½ teaspoon nutmeg
2 eggs
½ cup corn oil
1 teaspoon vanilla
2 large apples, peeled, cored and cut into chunks

Instructions:
Preheat the oven to 350°.

Combine the flour, baking soda, sugar, cinnamon and nutmeg in a large mixing bowl. Add the eggs, oil and vanilla, and mix well. Then stir in the apples.

Turn the batter into a greased baking pan and bake about 1 hour, or until the apples are soft and a toothpick inserted in the center of the cake comes out clean. Don't peek for the first 15 minutes of baking.

Carrot Cake

Special Equipment:
8″ square or 9″ round baking pan, greased

Ingredients:
1 cup flour
1 teaspoon baking powder
1 teaspoon baking soda
1 teaspoon cinnamon
1 cup brown sugar
⅔ cup salad oil
2 eggs
1 to 1½ cups grated fresh carrots
8-ounce can crushed pineapple, drained
½ cup chocolate bits (optional)
½ cup chopped nuts (optional)

Instructions:
Preheat the oven to 350°.

Combine the flour, baking powder, baking soda, cinnamon and brown sugar in a large mixing bowl. Add the eggs and oil, and mix well. Stir in the carrots, pineapple and, if desired, the chocolate bits and/or nuts.

Turn the batter into a greased baking pan and bake 40 to 45 minutes, or until a toothpick inserted in the center of the cake comes out clean. Don't peek during the first 15 minutes of baking.

Chocolate Cake

Special Equipment:
9″ × 13″ baking pan, ungreased

Ingredients:
3 cups flour
2 cups sugar
6 tablespoons unsweetened cocoa
2 teaspoons baking soda
2 cups cold water
¾ cup salad oil
2 tablespoons vinegar
2 teaspoons vanilla

Instructions:
Preheat the oven to 350°.

Combine all the ingredients in a large bowl, then mix well with a large spoon until the batter is smooth.

Pour the batter into an ungreased baking pan. Bake about 40 minutes, or until a toothpick pushed into the center of the cake comes out clean. Don't peek during the first 15 minutes of baking.

Cut it into squares and serve right from the pan.

Squares

This very easy and delicious brownie recipe is mixed right in the saucepan. It can be cut into 25 small brownies.

Brownies

Special Equipment:
8-cup saucepan
8" square baking pan, well greased

Ingredients:
2 squares (2 ounces) unsweetened baking chocolate
⅓ cup shortening (butter or margarine)
1 cup sugar
2 eggs
⅔ cup flour
½ teaspoon baking powder
1 teaspoon vanilla
½ cup chopped walnuts

Instructions:
Preheat the oven to 350°.

Melt the chocolate and the shortening in a saucepan over very low heat, and then remove the pan from the stove.

Add the sugar and then the eggs to the chocolate mixture in the saucepan, stirring well after each addition. Combine the flour and the baking powder, add them to the chocolate mixture, and mix well. Then stir in the vanilla and the walnuts.

Spread the batter in a greased baking pan and bake 25 to 30 minutes, or until a toothpick inserted in the center comes out clean.

Cool in the pan, then cut into 25 small brownies.

COOKIES

Two Candylike Oatmeal Cookies That You Don't Even Have to Bake

These recipes each make about 100 cookies that can be frozen or stored in an airtight tin. You can, of course, make only half a recipe.

Peanut Butter Oatmeal Cookies

Special Equipment:
8-cup saucepan
Waxed paper

Ingredients:
½ cup shortening (butter or margarine)
2 cups sugar
½ cup milk
2 teaspoons vanilla
3 heaping tablespoons peanut butter
3 cups uncooked oatmeal

Instructions:
Put the shortening, sugar and milk into a saucepan, and then place over low heat. Heat until the shortening melts and bubbles appear on the top of the mixture to show it has come to a boil. Boil for 2 minutes, then turn off the heat and remove the pan from the stove.

Add the vanilla, peanut butter and oatmeal to the ingredients in the saucepan, and stir until well mixed.

Place a large sheet of waxed paper on a counter top or other flat surface. Then drop teaspoonfuls of the oatmeal mixture onto the waxed paper and allow the cookies to cool and set for 2 to 3 hours.

Chocolate Oatmeal Cookies

Special Equipment:
8-cup saucepan
Waxed paper

Ingredients:
½ cup shortening (butter or margarine)
2 cups sugar
½ cup milk
¼ cup unsweetened cocoa
¾ cup chopped walnuts
3 cups uncooked oatmeal
1 teaspoon vanilla

Instructions:
Combine the shortening, sugar, milk and cocoa in a saucepan, and then place the pan over low heat. Heat until the mixture comes to a rolling boil. Boil for 1 minute, then turn off the heat and remove the pan from the stove.

Add the walnuts, oatmeal and vanilla to the ingredients in the saucepan, and then stir until well mixed.

Place a large sheet of waxed paper on a counter top or other flat surface. Then drop teaspoonfuls of the oatmeal mixture onto the waxed paper. Allow the cookies to cool and set for 2 to 3 hours.

Candies

Nut Brittle

Special Equipment:
Heavy 4-cup saucepan
Cookie sheet, greased

Ingredients:
1 cup sugar
½ cup coarsely chopped peanuts, almonds or cashews

Instructions:
Put the sugar into a heavy saucepan and place the pan over low heat. Heat, stirring all the time, until the sugar has melted into a clear syrup. Then turn off the heat and remove the pan from the stove.

Add the nuts to the saucepan and stir until they are all coated with the syrup.

Drop the mixture by teaspoonfuls onto a greased cookie sheet or pour the mixture onto the cookie sheet in a thin layer and break the candy into pieces after it cools. It will harden very quickly into brittle.

Hawaiian Jellies

Special Equipment:
4-cup saucepan
8″ square baking pan, greased

Ingredients:
4 envelopes (4 tablespoons) unflavored gelatin
⅓ cup sugar
2 cups canned pineapple juice
⅓ cup shredded coconut

Instructions:
Combine the gelatin and sugar in a mixing bowl. In a saucepan, heat the pineapple juice to the boiling point. Then pour the hot juice into the bowl and stir until the gelatin and sugar are completely dissolved. Pour the mixture into a greased baking pan and sprinkle with the shredded coconut.

Place the pan in the refrigerator and chill until the jelly is firm.

To serve, cut the jelly into small squares. The squares do not have to be refrigerated after they are firm.

Apple Jelly Squares

Special Equipment:
4-cup saucepan
8″ square baking pan, greased

Ingredients:
4 envelopes (4 tablespoons) unflavored gelatin
¼ cup sugar
2½ cups apple juice
⅓ cup chopped walnuts

Instructions:
Combine the gelatin and sugar in a medium-sized mixing bowl. In a saucepan, heat the apple juice to the boiling point. Pour the hot juice into the mixing bowl and stir until the gelatin and sugar are completely dissolved. Then pour the mixture into a greased baking pan and sprinkle with the chopped nuts.

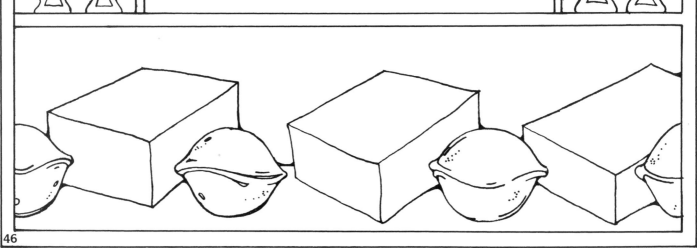